LILIAN REAM
: a life in photography

Biographical material by

Violet Fosbrook-Ream

Designed and Edited by

David Rayner

Research by

Kim Bowden

Cambridgeshire
County Council

Libraries & Information Service

Published by:
Cambridgeshire County Council
Libraries & Information Service
Babbage House
Shire Hall
Cambridge CB3 0AP

ISBN 1 870724 82 8

Typeset by Cambridgeshire Libraries Resources Unit,
        19 Gordon Avenue, March PE15 8AL

Printed by :
Balding + Mansell plc
Park Works
Park Road
Wisbech
Cambs   PE13 2AX

Acknowledgements

A number of the Ream family photographs have been kindly provided by Mrs Violet Fosbrook Ream from her private collection

The other photographs used in this book have been printed by Andrew Ingram and Anna Oakford from original negatives

Additional information provided by:
Betty Curwood and Dorothy Clydesdale, both nee Humphrey, who worked for the Studio, Andrew Ingram George MacDonald, Roger Van Hinsberg and Mrs Peggy Welbourne

* *

Lilian Ream Collection
District Library
Ely Place
Wisbech
Cambs   PE13 1EU

Telephone: 0945 64009
Fax: 0945 582784

CONTENTS

The dates included in some of the captions are only approximate. If you can supply any further information please contact the Lilian Ream Collection at Wisbech Library.

****

Many of the negatives suffer from staining or cracked and damaged emulsion. Where these have been used in the book they have been deliberately left unretouched in order to illustrate the condition of the collection.

1 EARLY LIFE

John Thomas and Louisa Pratt both came from farming families living in West Walton. They were married in 1860 and the first of their eight children was born the next year. Their youngest daughter was born on 30th June 1877 and she was called Lilian.

Details of Lilian's childhood are sketchy but we know that she was educated at Miss Bradley's private school in Wisbech Castle. She was a precocious child, showing signs of both her creative nature and her forceful personality. When she was ten years old she made a little office, in the cupboard under the stairs, where she would write short poems and articles for a weekly children's religious newspaper, called "The Little Gleaner". Her brother, Tom, well remembered her tendency to fly into tempers in order to get her own way - a trait that continued throughout her life.

In 1894, at the age of seventeen, Lilian started work as a photographic apprentice to Alfred Drysdale, whose studio was situated on Lynn Road, Wisbech. The Studio had been started by the younger Valentine Blanchard in the 1880's. When Blanchard moved to Cambridge the studio was sold, first to John Hinley and then to Drysdale.

Lilian Pratt, as a young girl, photographed by Edward Johnson.

She stayed with the firm when it was taken over by Hardingham Mehew and Leonard Smith. Smith was best know for his feats in goal for Wisbech Town Football Club and spent much of his time trying to produce a large painting showing all the team's players in action but this was apparently never finished!

Lilian moved on to continue her training under John Kennerell, a photographer and framemaker who operated from the Borough Studio in York Row. During this period she learned all the skills of her trade, from using a camera, developing negatives and making prints, to hand colouring and framing.

John Kennerell was one of a number of photographers working in Wisbech at the time, who also included Edward Johnson and George Swaine. The Borough Studio was a large shop with living accommodation above and a small cottage in the gardens, which ran down to Alexandra Road. The studio and darkroom were connected to the shop by a dark passageway known as "Ghost Passage", which was reputedly haunted by a member of the Peckover family.

All the local studios concentrated on portraiture, producing large numbers of the formal individual and family portraits which seem to typify the Victorian middle class.

It is interesting to realise that much of the stiffness was the result of the need to hold the pose for several seconds due to the long exposure times of the early cameras. The Borough Studio even used a special chair with a small neck clamp to ensure stillness. Cameras were large and heavy, needing a strong tripod to hold them steady. Glass plates, coated with a gelatine silver bromide emulsion, were placed in the camera and the negative image would be formed on them. As these were so large most cameras could only hold them singly with the camera needing to be reloaded between each shot. The negative image was formed within the light sensitive emulsion and the glass acted only as a support to the microscopically thin and extremely delicate film which adhered to its surface.

John Kennerell seems to have had a number of partners, starting with a man called Beales at a shop in 8 and 9 High Street, Wisbech. He was working on his own at the Borough Studio at the time Lilian Pratt joined him. Soon after the turn of the century, the business was taken over by Lawrence Brown who, in 1908, made Lilian, then his manageress, a partner. However the partnership did not include an increase in salary and the resultant dispute led not only to Lilian's resignation but to a long and sometimes bitter rivalry.

MY PET CAT JET.

WHEN I was a very little girl I had a cat named Jet, which used to play and frolic about with me like a dog. I taught it to do many little tricks, and being very intelligent, it quickly learnt them. It regularly came up stairs for me every morning, and tapped at my bedroom door, showing its affection by jumping on my lap, and trying to rub itself against my face. When it first came to us, it was a very thin, starved little kitten, and must have been a stray one, for it used to make its home in an old disused shed we had, till one morning I took a fancy to it, and afterwards it was always styled "Lillian's cat." Jet used to follow me nearly to the town, and did not seem at all to fear meeting dogs on the way. There was a dog that used to come and was quite a bother to us through running away with things. But soon after Jet came, we were not bothered at all, for she would sit on the step and watch for the thief, who, when it appeared, she would show her entire disapproval by spitting and clawing in a manner which soon made him run howling away. Although this seems funny for a cat to do, it is quite true. Often we used to see Jet up in a tree (which was close to our house) with a dog at the bottom, vainly trying to conquer Jet, but without success. It was quite amusing to see her sitting quite quietly on the branches, blinking her eyes in the sun, and taking no notice whatever of the discomfited enemy below. When I was big enough to go to school, Jet, knowing she must not follow me, used to perch herself on the garden railings and watch me down the road, until she could not see me. One of Jet's kittens is living now, or rather a cat, and is as big as its mother.

LILLIAN PRATT

Wisbech.   (Aged 13½ years).

Extract from "The Little Gleaner".   1890.

Alfred Drysdale's portrait of Lilian, aged about 17.

The Borough Studio when owned by John Kennerell at the turn of the century.

Lilian and Sydney Ream on their wedding day, Photographed by Lawrence Brown. 25th January 1905.

TOWN SCENES

Wisbech is situated at the centre of a web of farming communities and has developed as a busy commercial centre. The conjunction of rich farmland, with access to the sea, has been vital to Wisbech's development and is reflected in the rich variety of images preserved in the Lilian Ream Collection.

The Studio's photographers vividly captured the bustle of the prosperous Market Place and the gaiety of celebratory parades as well as the contrasting narrow back streets and the grim reality of rationing.

Two of the Lilian Ream Studio's most important customers were the local newspapers, the Wisbech Standard and the Wisbech and Isle of Ely Advertiser. This work included recording the everyday sights and important events during a period which saw many changes in both the structure of the town and the activities of the inhabitants.

High Street, Wisbech. Late 1920's.

Shopping Week parade, Wisbech Market Place.   1927.   These were regularly organised by the Chamber of Trade in order to promote the town.

Church Terrace, Wisbech.   1928.

Chapel Road, Wisbech.   1946.

Wisbech Shire Horse Society's spring parade of stallions at the Cattle Market. 1936.

Parade to celebrate the Jubilee of King George V and Queen Mary, Bridge Street, Wisbech.   May 1935.

10

Ashworth's Yard - one of the small back streets off West Street, Wisbech.   1933.

During the severe winter of 1947, queues formed at Wisbech gas works to buy small amounts of coke to supplement the meagre fuel ration.

2 STARTING OUT

Lilian married Sydney Ream on 25th January 1905 and their first child, John Roland Fosbrook Ream, was born just over two years later. At first the couple lived in Lonsdale Terrace, Victoria Road, having been married in the nearby Zion Baptist Chapel. Domestic duties were not to Lilian's taste, she would employ others to deal with that side of life, leaving her free to pursue her own ambitions.

A combination of her disagreement with Lawrence Brown and changing family circumstances brought about Lilian's decision to start up on her own. There were protracted negotiations to dissolve the recently formed partnership but the break was made official on 9th April 1909. Meanwhile Lilian had taken a lease on 4 The Crescent and opened for business only eight days later. Sydney worked as a tailor, having served his apprenticeship in Savile Row, and his support was vital whilst Lilian was establishing her business.

As the family were to live in the new house, a studio was constructed in the garden. With a floor area of approximately 700 square feet, the studio also contained a darkroom, changing rooms and storage space. Mr. Southwell,

The Crescent Studio.

the landlord, would only allow this on the understanding that if the business was not a success within six months the studio would be demolished and every daisy replaced in the lawn!

Apparently many of the Crescent's residents were horrified at the intrusion of "commerce" into their select neighbourhood but soon the constant stream of local worthies, who arrived for portrait sittings, created sufficient excitement and gossip to calm their fears.

Lilian's older sister, Louie, was persuaded to leave her job in London in order to help her. The birth of Lilian's daughter, Mary, in 1911 was only a minor distraction - she left all domestic matters to Louie, the nanny and the other domestic help. Louie's burden was further increased when Lilian's parents moved into the household which, by this time, had been purchased outright. With this large extended family and the business, No 4 must have been very cramped and during the First World War, Louie was able to talk Lilian into buying No 5. The family moved next door, giving the children a garden to play in and allowing their old house to be totally devoted to the studio.

Lilian and Sydney with Roland and Mary. 1914.

Lilian with the staff of the Crescent Studio.

Lilian with Roland and Mary in 1911.
A skillfully blended composite portrait made from two different negatives.

VILLAGE SCENES

Although based in Wisbech the Studio also served all the surrounding villages. The firm was often hired to take photographs at private parties and weddings, particularly at the homes of wealthy local landowners.

The Studio's photographers also recorded the many events which are so important in the life of a small, tightly knit, village community. Local people were rightly proud of the opening of new schools, chapels and village halls and wanted a record of the event.

All local villages held summer fetes to raise money for charity. Some of the larger events attracted people from a wide area and often included professional performers.

The start of the Wisbech canal at Outwell Sluice. 1929.

A classroom scene in the new school at West Walton which was opened in April 1927.

The Mayor of Wisbech, Alderman Reginald Curston, tops up the new swimming pool at Fridaybridge school.
September 1965.

Chase-water Charlie, a clown from Truro in Cornwall, performing at Murrow sports.   1931.

3 THE CRESCENT STUDIO

The Crescent Studio proved to be an outstanding success. Like other photographic businesses of the time, its prosperity was based on portraiture. The best possible results were essential if the business was to thrive and so, for the new Studio, Lilian had purchased a camera, with a first class Dallmeyer portrait lens, which remained her favourite for nearly twenty years.

The quality of Lilian's work attracted a high profile clientele which ensured the Studio's reputation would spread. Among the sitters were Mr and Mrs James de Rothschild, the local Liberal MP, members of the Peckover family and the then Bishop of Ely. Each year the Mayor of Wisbech attended the Studio for an official portrait. The series lasted from 1909 to 1971 and the results were always displayed in the Studio window. The official portrait required the official chair. It was extremely heavy but had to be carried from the Council Chamber, for over two hundred yards across the Town Bridge, by the Town Beadle and his helpers. This was not a popular task!

Her many other sitters also posed with a variety of props and in front of skillfully painted backdrops. Children were given toys to hold or play with and it was not unknown for the Ream children to find their new Christmas and birthday presents had been "borrowed" for the Studio.

Lilian would also take on outside photographic assignments such as weddings, garden parties and special events. She cycled everywhere loaded down with her heavy camera case, which also contained the glass plates in their holders, a black velvet bag to hold the exposed negatives and a large black velvet cloth to cover the camera and her head. In addition a folded wooden tripod was strapped to the cycle and she would be ready for anything. Her dedication was such that on one occasion she left her Christmas dinner to cycle to Sutton Bridge in order to photograph a client's party!

With the outbreak of the Great War Sydney joined theRoyal Naval Air Service and spent most of the war with the Dover Patrol, which protected the vital convoys of men and supplies across the Channel.

For security reasons travel to the south coast was restricted and although Lilian had a special permit to visit she often made use of her cousin's London flat so that she and Sydney could make the most of his short leaves. Her cousin, Evelyn Merriken-Smith, became a well known figure in the world of dance. She ran a ballet school in Norwich and their common interest in the arts made them great friends.

The business continued to grow and by 1916 Lilian was so busy that she arranged for Roland and Mary to stay with her sister, Millie, in Hastings. This meant that not only was Louie available to help in the Studio, but one of Millie's older daughters, Muriel, was also dispatched to Wisbech to work in the family enterprise. No matter what the circumstances the Studio always came first.

With the ending of the war life returned to normal. Sydney returned to tailoring and Louie resumed her domestic tasks. Lilian was quite content with this arrangement as long as she could spend her time in the Studio or attending the outdoor functions and weddings which formed such a big part of the work.

In summer, when the Studio closed for half days, the family would go boating. The rest of the party would travel to Upwell on the tramway but Lilian would cycle and was often known to arrive first. Increasing prosperity brought first a motor cycle and sidecar and then a motor car - a coupe with a dickie seat for the children, who had to hope it didn't rain!

Lilian's First World War permit to travel to the South Coast.

Lilian with Sydney, who served in the Royal Naval Air Service, 1914-18.

Sydney, wearing his flying kit, when serving with the Dover Patrol.

Lilian working at her desk in the Crescent Studio.

24

WORK

During the period in which the Lilian Ream Studio operated Wisbech was a small market town serving a large
rural catchment area. This was reflected in the way in
which most employment was either connected to agriculture or to providing services to the inhabitants of the
area. All the essential requirements of the farming community from forks to combine harvesters could be purchased from local suppliers. Crops could be harvested
into locally made baskets and boxes before being proc-
essed in local canning and jam making factories.

One exception to the agricultural connection is the
printing industry. Wisbech has a long tradition of fine
printing and the two main firms, Balding and Mansell
and Buralls, both celebrate their centenary in 1992.

Many local firms employed Lilian Ream to record their
buildings, equipment and staff, particularly at times of
change. Products were photographed for use in cata-
logues and advertisements leaving an excellent record of
local manufacture.

*Alf Riches, the town rat catcher, displays his success.
Late 1920's.*

War work - assembling munitions boxes at English Brothers factory.   1944.

Smedley's vegetable canning factory.   1931.

When unloading timber, dock workers would carry it up sloping planks to the top of stacks in the adjacent timber yards. 1933.

Cyril Hookham, guillotine operator at the Wisbech printers, Balding & Mansell. 1950.

G.P.O. sorting office, Wisbech.   1935.

Smith's shop, Elizabeth Terrace, Wisbech. Late 1950's.

Mrs Amelia Harley (88), an employee of Horace Friend for 47 years, sorts pheasant tail feathers for export to world fashion houses. 1954.

4 THE BUSINESS GROWS

As Lilian's business had grown, that of Lawrence Brown had declined. He sank into deeper financial difficulties but refused to sell to his ambitious and gifted rival. When he could carry on no longer the premises were purchased by Colonel Ollard, a solicitor, whose offices were in the next property. The Colonel altered the first floor to provide extra space for his own business but had no use for the rest.

Lilian saw the chance to achieve her greatest ambition and persuaded the new owner to lease her the Borough Studio. She soon had a string of businesses across the town. To her Crescent properties and the Borough Studio she added The Art Studio in Alexandra Road which was previously a branch of Jasper Wright's of King's Lynn. She ran this as a framing works under the title "The Burlington Studio". She would not tolerate competition and took over the Imperial Photo Company, at 50 Market Place, from Mr H Coates and Sons, who were allowed to continue to operate as postcard publishers. A craft shop in Market Street was added to the collection and she also bought out her first employers, at the Lynn Road Studio, keeping Leonard Smith as an assistant until she moved the business to the Borough Studio.

Lilian could not proceed with her plans to fulfil the potential of the Borough Studio without the freehold. She made such a nuisance of herself with the Ollards that eventually they gave in and she became the proud owner.

The Colonel insisted on retaining his new first floor offices and Lilian had to reluctantly accept this. The entrance was altered to give an arcade of windows leading into the main shop. One side of the arcade was kept for her own use and the other, with a self-contained showroom was let to a ladies outfitters. At the rear, the cottage was demolished and new showrooms for bric-a-brac and craft displays were built. A new studio and workshop with dressing rooms, darkrooms and negative storage were reached across a small paved garden. A large flat was also built over the showrooms facing Alexandra Road.

When all the work was completed Lilian gathered the various businesses under one roof; the Market Street and Market Place shops were let and, in 1928, 4 The Crescent was turned into flats.

As if all this disruption was not enough, Lilian fell in love with 6 North Brink when it came on the market and she quickly bought it. It was a superb Georgian house with a particularly fine staircase and a large garden with palm trees, figs, peaches and roses, leading down to stables and garages which opened onto Chapel Road.

Louie, of course, ran the new house, with a staff of two live-in maids, a daily char and Mr Moon, the gardener, who worked for the family for forty-seven years. Once the family had moved in, 5 The Crescent was also turned into flats.

Meanwhile the children had been growing up. Mary went first to the Wisbech High School for girls and then away to Highfield School at Gorleston. Roland attended Wisbech Grammar School and wanted to be a chemist but when he was sixteen his tutor died and he left school to join the family firm.

Sydney had also been persuaded to give up tailoring and now everyone's lives were bound up with the Borough Studio.

On a trip to Hastings Lilian and Roland had a very lucky escape when a fifteen ton lorry, loaded with granite chips, skidded on a wet road and crushed the front of their car. Lilian, who was in the front passenger seat, escaped with cuts and bruises and Roland was luckier still. As the lorry sliced right over the driver's seat he managed to slide to the floor. After being rescued Roland calmly photographed the wreckage.

PORTRAITS

Before the age of cheap, lightweight cameras many people would visit their local photographic studio regularly. Childhood and coming of age, marriage and parenthood, birthdays and anniversaries, a new job and improved circumstances were all occasions to be captured and preserved in the family photograph album.

Portraiture was the basis of the Lilian Ream Studio which could not survive without the steady income it brought in.

Sitters would pose before stunningly realistic painted backdrops with a variety of skilfully positioned props. These could range from toys for the children to stone pillars, tables and ornately carved chairs for the adults. In the early days lighting would have been by natural daylight from north facing windows. Later flash and studio lights were added but these were always used in a subtle manner to bring out the best in the sitter's features. Before printing, many portraits would also be retouched to remove skin blemishes and lines. A customer who was flattered by their portrait was a customer for life.

Baby Hawes photographed on 7th May 1924.

Mary Ream. 1920.

Master Frear poses with the Studio's pedal car. 1928.

Mr Gaskin in a typical pose of the period. 1930's.

*Trooper Copeland of the 17th Lancers strikes
a more martial attitude.*

Portrait of Miss Howard.   1920's.

Miss Hickman.   1933.

The wedding of Dr Harry L Groom, Medical Officer of Health for Wisbech, and Miss Inez Metcalfe Aycliffe.
6th September 1929.

The Hicks family at the time of the Great War.

Councillor J K and Mrs Mellor, Mayor and Mayoress of Wisbech in 1944. Councillor Mellor won the Military Medal for bravery at the battle of the Somme in 1916.

Mrs Corley with her dog.   1958.

Mr and Mrs Shippey celebrate their diamond wedding anniversary.   1935.

5 | THE BOROUGH STUDIO

The Borough Studio was soon established as a thriving business providing a variety of services. The photographic side of the business was complemented by the sale of craft materials. It was often necessary for the staff to give demonstrations in their use and lessons in various artistic techniques.

Lilian's presence was all pervading. She was the heart and soul of the business, which dominated her life. She supervised every aspect of the work of the Studio while still taking many of the photographs herself. Much of her time was spent visiting potential clients and in maintaining her contacts in the local business community.

During these years the firms manager was Alan Midlane, whose hard work was as invaluable as his calm nature, which had to survive his employer's many temperamental outbursts. One of his responsibilities was to select photographs for use by both local newspapers and it was no easy task to keep the rival editors happy but he always did.

A whole team of photographers and darkroom assistants was joined by retouchers, watercolourists and sales staff.

Such was Lilian Ream's reputation as a teacher there was no shortage of applicants for apprenticeships with the firm. Lilian worked non stop herself and expected others to do the same.

The Studio was open from 9.00am to 7.00pm four days a week, from 9.00am to lunchtime one day a week and from 9.00am to 8.00pm every Saturday. Apprentices worked all these hours except for an hour for lunch - a fifty hour week - with two weeks holiday per year. Those joining the firm in 1929 did so to learn a trade and, as they were guaranteed excellent tuition in their chosen craft, they were not paid any salary at all. By 1938 an apprentice could expect to receive the grand sum of 1/3d (6.25p) per week pocket money. During the summer the firm's girls had to wear black and white striped dresses which were the Kodak trademark and in winter, brown smocks with large bows. Lilian was a hard taskmaster, enforcing the highest standards, but her perfectionism earned her the respect of all her staff and pupils.

One of the most fascinating aspects of the Studio's work was the retouching and colouring. In order to flatter customers, scalpels and soft pencils would be used to remove or blot out wrinkles and skin blemishes on the actual negative. The negative would then be printed and improved still further with paint before being rephotographed to provide a much improved image. Even farmers insisted on the improvement of their prized livestock. For instance extra "body" would be added to negatives of cattle in order to straighten the line of their backs.

Most colouring was by hand, using watercolours and fine brushes, although large background areas would be coloured using a small spray, called an aerograph, which had to be pumped by foot to maintain the air pressure. Many of the surviving negative bags include instructions on the colour of clothes, eyes, hair and jewellery and sometimes contain samples of cloth and hair.

Portraits of children would often have the background completely blanked out so that small rabbits and flowers could be painstakingly added by hand.

The firm also took many thousands of photographs outside the Studio of people and events. These included fascinating scenes of local agriculture, industry and leisure activities.

Lilian was closely involved in the staging of the 1929 pageant, when the visit of King John to Wisbech in 1216 was re-enacted by 951 actors using a script devised by Arthur Bryant. During the preparations Lilian entertained Arthur and his assistant, Maisie Marshall, who constantly met with Aunt Louie's disapproval by feeding her Alsatian dog large bones under the dining table. Arthur Bryant went on to become famous as an author and historian, receiving a knighthood in 1954. Apart from taking hundreds of photographs of the occasion, the firm also made the first 16mm cine film of a local event.

The local amateur operatic society was another source of custom. After their weekend dress rehearsal the cast would wander through the town in full costume so that their portraits could be taken in the Studio. This was a popular sight for the townspeople but back in the days of the Crescent Studio these Sunday visitors had to be slipped in very quietly so as not to alert Lilian's strictly Baptist mother.

The firm gained permission, through the Head Gardener, to take a series of photographs of the gardens at Sandringham House. These were then hand coloured, which was a very exacting task as they had to be perfect. The firms head artist had to visit the gardens and note the colour of every bloom. A selection of photographs was chosen by Queen Mary, whose pleasure was passed on to Lilian by one of her Ladies in Waiting.

AGRICULTURE

Before drainage the fens were a mixture of marshland, rough grazing and open water, or meres, with a scattering of "islands" of slightly higher ground. In the seventeenth century Dutch engineers, financed by wealthy merchants and aristocrats, began a series of drainage works which have resulted in todays flat open landscape, criss-crossed by dykes and waterways, which forms some of the richest farmland in the country.

Modern intensive farming has led to even greater production, but also to great change, including a dramatic decrease in the number of people working on the land.

Apart from the local people, whole families would travel from London for the summer fruit harvest. They would live in bunk house accommodation on outlying farms and the children would be cared for by students from Cambridge University while their parents worked.

As well as potatoes, sugarbeet and cereal crops the area is noted for its fruit and, reflecting the Dutch influence, bulbs and flowers.

Harvest scene at West Walton. 1960.

Picking pyrethrum flowers at Payne's farm.   1933.

Bunching daffodils for the Easter market at Bath's farm, West Walton. Early 1930's.

London fruit pickers arriving at the Great Eastern station, Victoria Road, Wisbech.   1930.

Fruit pickers at Ayres bunkhouse, Redmoor Camp, Elm.   1931.

Potato picking gang. 1930.

Harvesting wheat with a horse drawn reaper/binder.

An International Farmall Regulator tractor hauling a McCormick power take-off reaper/binder on the Coldham Estate.

6 ADVERSITY STRIKES

On 25th January 1930 Lilian and Sydney celebrated their Silver Wedding with a party at their North Brink home. After all her years of hard work the business was thriving and she was an established figure in local society. With the household smoothly run by Louie she could spend all her time immersed in the Borough Studio - "her baby"! There seemed to be not a cloud on the horizon but soon all was to be shattered by a series of personal tragedies.

Lilian's concentration on work led to her becoming increasingly detached from her family, who she nevertheless expected to be at her side whenever she could spare them the time. The whole family worked in the Borough Studio but there was no escape out of work hours. During the summer the family would visit Heacham, where they had a beach hut, but even there Lilian could not avoid talking about work and even took negatives along for retouching.

On a visit to her sister, in Hastings, Louie suffered a heart attack and died. Lilian's grief was deepened by the knowledge of how much she had relied upon her sister. A cousin of Lilian's now began to visit the house and was drawn into helping to run the establishment. At Lilian's

suggestion Sydney would take the new recruit home if she stayed late into the evening. Thrown together in this way it was not surprising that romance blossomed between the two, whilst Lilian continued to ignore everything outside the business. Eventually Lilian realised the depth of feeling between her husband and cousin. The shock, for once, undermined her formidable fighting spirit and she decided to retire to Eastbourne to be near her sister Millie.

Of course Lilian still insisted on arranging everyone's lives. Her arrangements included Sydney and Roland moving into the flat above the Borough Studio, with Mary accompanying her mother to their new home at 38 Upper Avenue, Eastbourne. There Mary met and married the son of a family whose garden adjoined theirs.

Meanwhile, in Wisbech, the business was to be run by Sydney and Roland with Alan Midlane doing the outside work and framing and Hugh Bennett managing the Studio and darkrooms. A team of other staff dealt with developing and printing, colouring and retouching.

At first Lilian seemed to enjoy life in Eastbourne, joining several local societies and taking up a number of hobbies. In particular she developed her talent for embroidery, producing a number of excellent tapestries. She also learnt to drive and passed her test first time, although not without mishap - including ignoring a policeman's signal to halt whilst on her test!

While living in Eastbourne she suffered a further blow with the death of her cousin and friend Evelyn Neal (nee Merriken-Smith). Evelyn was only forty three years old when she died from pneumonia caught during rehearsals for a ballet performance which was to have brought the great Alicia Markova to Norwich.

Lilian Ream. Approximately 1930.

The Borough Studio staff. 1929.

Front row (l. to r.) Alan Midlane, ? , Roland Ream, Lilian Ream, Sydney Ream, Mary Ream, Cyril Hopkins.

Middle row ? , Dorothy Humphrey, ? , ? , ? , ? , Stanley Eagle. Back row ? , Hugh Bennett, ?

Borough Studio staff wearing their summer "Kodak" dresses. 1960's.

Mary Ream hand tinting a photograph. 1929.

TRANSPORT

The lifetime of the Lilian Ream Studio saw a revolution in transport. The horses and barges of an earlier age were slowly replaced by private cars and heavy lorries. Even the style of these newcomers was subject to constant and rapid alteration due to technological advances and changing fashion.

One feature of the transport network in this region was its close relationship with agriculture. Fresh produce needed to be moved quickly and cheaply from the fields to the markets and in the first half of the century a variety of means was used to do this. After harvest, crops could be taken a relatively short distance to a waterway for transport by barge or to one of the many stops on the Upwell to Wisbech tramway. Transport firms also established depots for the collection and rapid distribution of fruit both to market and to canning and jam making factories.

Carting apples at Herrod's farm. 1931.

The Wisbech to Upwell tram crosses Elm Road. The diesel locomotive is a Drewry diesel mechanical 060 shunter, no.2201. 1966.

Loading sugar beet on to a fenland lighter at Nordelph.   1933.

Strawberry collection depot at Bert Fillingham's yard, West Walton. 1951.

7 A NEW START

Lilian was still only 58 years old, far too young for someone of her energy to retire. Once her daughter Mary had married she returned to Wisbech to check on the running of the business and was unable to resist the urge to take up the reins again.

She could not forgive Sydney and they had a final separation but divorce was not possible for her - it would have been an admission of failure! Thus it was arranged that Sydney would receive the rents of one of the Crescent properties, which enabled him to live at the White Lion Hotel until his death in 1950. The depth of the rift between them can be seen in the stipulation in Sydney's will that Lilian was not to attend his funeral. He had also become cut off from the rest of the family, refusing to meet Roland and his wife, Violet, or any of his grandchildren.

Sydney appears to have been overshadowed by his formidable wife but he led an active life outside the Borough Studio and his popularity was shown by the hundreds of people who attended his funeral, including guards of honour formed by representatives of both the RAF Association and the Isle of Ely Special Constables.

After her return, in 1935, Lilian and Roland lived in the Borough Studio flat. A year later Roland married Violet Seaman and took her on honeymoon to the south coast in the British racing green MG sports car of which he was so proud. There she could be inspected and approved by various relatives.

During this trip the couple received the news that a horse, drawing a coal wagon belonging to Roland's best man, had run amok in the High Street and had careered into the plate glass windows of the Borough Studio. Their wedding photographs had been on display and were totally ruined - Violet is still waiting for them to be reprinted!

Lilian arranged for the newlyweds to live in the flat and it was a great surprise to Violet when she returned from her honeymoon to find that she was expected to share with her mother-in-law and her Great-aunt Julia, Evelyn Merriken-Smith's mother. After the birth of their son, Roger, the young couple were delighted when Lilian decided that the flat was not big enough for a child and started house hunting on their behalf. She purchased 24 North Brink, which was large enough to provide separate living rooms for herself and Roland's family.

Lilian began to take a full part in the running of the

business, often attending weddings throughout the area. Brides were so pleased if Lilian personally took their wedding photgraphs that she would often be invited to join the reception guests on the top table. Apart from the normal work of the Studio, Roland was beginning to develop an interest in cine photography. He made many films of local events and was specially invited to make a film of a performance by Bertram Mills circus although photography was not normally allowed in the Big Top. The Studio also made a series of photographs and films of Peter Scott, who, in the late 1930's, lived in the East Lighthouse at Sutton Bridge where he executed many paintings of the migratory and native birds which frequent the coastal marshes.

The outbreak of the Second World War brought many changes. Roland joined the RAF and spent most of the war stationed in the West country. During the Blitz many children were evacuated from London to the relative safety of the countryside and Lilian agreed to take in four sisters, aged between five and twelve. Of course, once they arrived, Lilian left the care of the children to Violet except for a formal visit to her drawing room for half an hour each Sunday evening.

Many of the male staff were called up but Mr Midlane was too old for service and so was left to do all the outside photography. However, he couldn't drive and so Violet, despite the recent birth of her daughter, had to drive everywhere with Roger and the newlyborn Jennifer in the back. To help with her navigation, Violet would send details of their assignments to Roland, who would send back maps and notes on the route such as "turn left at the black barn" and "pass the house with the crooked chimmey."

The firm's huge collection of negatives suffered some damage when, in the winter of 1942, a fire broke out in the next door solictor's office. Lilian and Violet were called out in the early hours to find the dividing wall between the properties red hot. The heat and the gallons of water used to extinguish the fire caused many of the glass plates to crack. The fire brigade had to send Lilian home when they discovered her, at the height of the fire, struggling to rescue the *empty* cash register.

Lilian wanted Violet to work longer hours in the shop but she felt she could not leave Roger, who had been seriously ill, and Jennifer alone. Lilian's solution was to move her and her children back to the flat so that Violet would have no excuse. The end of the war coincided with the expiry of the lease on the family's old home. An exchange was arranged with the tenants, who moved to the Borough Studio flat, while Roland and Violet moved back to 6 North Brink and Lilian remained at No 24.

Once Roland had been demobbed he and Violet took on a greater share of the running of the Studio and in 1949, at the age of 72, Lilian decided to retire for good. She set up a limited company with Roland as Managing Director and Violet as Director and Secretary with shares being given to Mr Midlane and three other staff.

Having arranged everything to her own satisfaction Lilian finally retired to Eastbourne.

Roland Ream's Cine Service shop window. 1952.

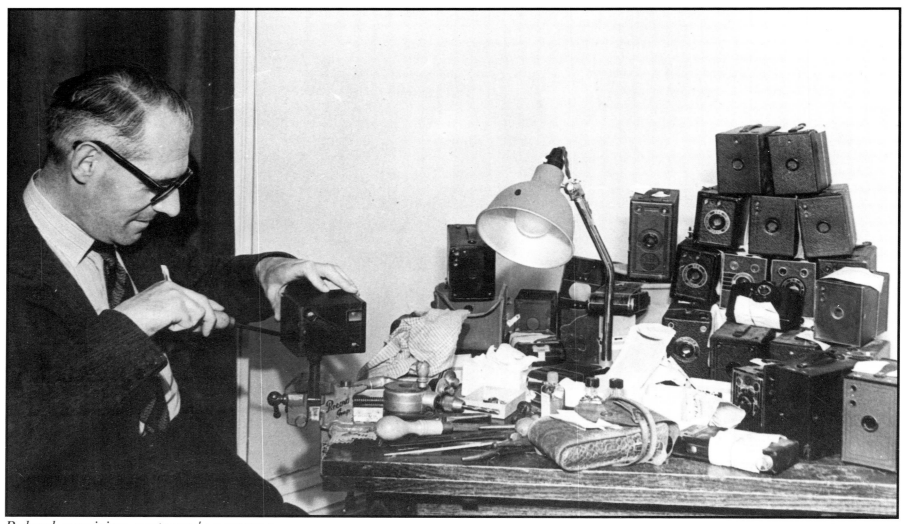

Roland repairing customer's cameras.

LEISURE

Fenland was famous for its skaters who could take on the best in the world. From Turkey Smart to Cyril Horn, the champions on their "Fen runners" have always been great characters.

The annual swimming races held in the river Nene at Wisbech were a popular event for over thirty years until their indefinite suspension in 1939. Competitors would enter the river from rowing boats, north of Wisbech, and race back to the finishing line near the Town Bridge where the waiting crowds would be entertained by displays of diving.

The arrival of the Mart was also eagerly awaited and its stalls and rides occupied large areas of the town. Street parties and parades were held to celebrate many events from Royal jubilees to victory in war. In 1929 the great Wisbech pageant "Heart of the Fens" was a tremendous success. The popularity of this type of event was reflected in the thriving amateur theatrical companies of the area including operatic and dramatic societies and Mrs Chesters' Little Theatre group.

Cyril Horn, champion ice skater, competing at Lingay Fen. 1933.

Roy Claxton diving into the river at Sutton Bridge, in September 1949, when he swam the eight miles to Wisbech to show that it would not be too dangerous to resume the traditional river races.

A scene from the 1929 pageant depicting the visit of King John to Wisbech in 1216.

"Miss Hook of Holland" performed by the Wisbech Amateur Dramatic Society at the Alexandra Theatre in 1931.

Mrs Chesters' Little Theatre Group, filmed by the BBC, performing in the grounds of Grammar School House, South Brink, Wisbech. 1957.

A popular ride at Wisbech Mart.   1930.

A street party, held in Prince Street, Wisbech, to celebrate Victory in 1945.

Listening to the Boat Race at the Wisbech Working Mens Club and Institute. Late 1920's.

8 RETIREMENT

Lilian settled down to a quieter life in Eastborne with a lady companion and housekeeper. She enjoyed an active retirement, taking regular drives around the Sussex countryside with her daughter or local friends. She also joined several local groups, including the Dickens Society.

Before she retired she had begun to suffer pains in the trigeminal nerve in her face. Tablets and a stay in a nursing home did not improve the problem and she remained in pain for the rest of her life.

She still visited Wisbech to check on the management of the rented properties she owned but found this increasingly burdensome. Visits to her family were more enjoyable, particularly the wedding of her grandson, Roger, in 1960.

Although in indifferent health Lilian was still active and enjoyed a drive with Mary, only two days before she died, aged 84, on Sunday 20th August 1961.

Her body was brought back from Eastbourne to Wisbech for burial in the Walsoken churchyard, just by the main

Lilian Ream pictured in St Peter's churchyard, Wisbech. 1951.

path. At her funeral the church was packed with mourners who heard fulsome tributes to this remarkable woman.

For a woman of her generation to found and run such a large and successful business, in a small provincial town, was in itself a significant achievement but her business success was equalled by her skill and artistry with a camera. Her hard businesslike approach and fiery temper made her a difficult person to work with but her professionalism and refusal to compromise on the highest standards engendered respect and admiration from many others. While she did not suffer fools gladly she must have inspired loyalty from her best staff as several remained with her all their working lives.

Lilian's single mindedness and capacity for hard work meant she would probably have succeeded in whatever enterprise she undertook. Wisbech is lucky that she chose a profession which has left such a superb record of the area and its people for future generations to enjoy.

Entrance to the Borough Studio with a special display for Shopping Week. 1951.

Interior of the Borough Studio shop.   1930's.

*Roland not only ran his own film shows but also sold or hired
the necessary projection equipment to others.*

9 ROLAND REAM

At the end of the war Roland had returned full of ideas for expanding the business in the field of cine films. In 1946 the lease on the separate dress shop had expired and he took it over as an independent business called "Roland Ream Cine Service". He had always been interested in cine photography and now was in the fortunate position of being able to build a business from his hobby.

The shop sold cine cameras and projectors, sold, developed and printed films and carried out equipment repairs. Schools from a wide area became important customers for the sale and maintenance of visual aid equipment. Roland also hired commercially produced films and would show them to local groups and at private parties. He was assisted by John Day who had previously worked for E. Lawrence Witcombe Ltd., the portrait and commercial photographers at 7 Nene Quay who were also accredited dealers for Gebescape and Pathe cine apparatus.

Roland went on to acquire a British-Thompson Housden 16mm sound projector which was a top quality machine. Before the advent of television in every home his shows were always extremely popular, with Laurel and Hardy being among the favourites. He also helped to found the Wisbech Film Society which hired mostly foreign films for its regular shows, which were held at Peckover House.

Meanwhile Violet expanded the craft side of the business into a very profitable sideline. At first she sold wool, tapestry kits and knitting machines but eventually specialised in babywear and converted part of the shop into the popular "Spinning Wheel Baby Boutique".

As more and more families acquired cheap, simple to use cameras so the formal studio portrait became a thing of the past. Anyone could take their own family snaps at home or on holiday and, although they would still have formal photographs taken at weddings, this was not enough to support the business.

The firm struggled on, and Roger became the third generation to enter the family business, but by 1971 Roland's health was in decline and the decision to close was taken. Roland and Violet retired to Hunstanton, where Violet still lives since her husband's death in 1988. Roland's body was laid to rest in the churchyard of Walsoken All Saints where he had been Rector's warden for 25 years.

Violet and Roland with their children Jennifer and Roger. 1952.

10 THE LILIAN REAM COLLECTION

The vast collection of negatives, which the Studio had accumulated, including over 15,000 purchased from earlier photographers, remained in the empty shop for ten years. Then, having suffered another fire and an unauthorised move, those which survived were purchased by Cambridgeshire Libraries. The Ream family accepted only a nominal sum as they were glad to see the collection in safe hands. Prior to the purchase by the Library a large number of negatives were removed from the shop without the permission of the Reams. Some have since been acquired by the Library but others are still in private hands. Their loss, along with the many thousands of negatives which have been broken or damaged over the years is a great tragedy for the town.

Nevertheless the Library now holds over 100,000 negatives, with the earliest, which can be definitely dated, taken in 1907. Many of the negatives are in very poor condition and a major programme of conservation work is urgently needed.

For several years a Manpower Services Commission funded scheme, sponsored by Fenland District Council, worked to sort the negatives from the complete jumble which had resulted from their unauthorised movement. The project also organised a number of small exhibitions which were always popular.

When the project ended the collection was returned to Wisbech Library where it is now housed. Since then the Library staff have been working on refining the categorisation of the negatives and preparing albums of prints for public inspection.

In November 1991 the Library borrowed an empty shop, in the Town Centre, to stage an exhibition of over five hundred photographs from the collection. The public response was quite staggering - in three weeks over seven thousand visitors enjoyed the chance to look back on the changing face of Wisbech and the Fens.

The negatives are of a number of different types, from early glass plates to 35mm safety film. Dampness, both from poor storage and the soaking many received when the fire brigade tackled fires in 1942 and 1981 has caused many stains and marks. Many glass plates have cracked or broken and the gelatine emulsion on nearly half the collection is becoming brittle and beginning to crack and flake away.

Conservation measures can arrest this deterioration but handling the negatives is a constant problem. The Library hopes to start a copying programme shortly but this will take many years and be extremely costly.

Income for the collection is generated by the sale of prints, postcards and books, but much more money is needed. Past exhibitions have been generously supported by local sponsors and the Library welcomes any offer of sponsorship or other financial support. The future of the collection is far from secure, it is physically deteriorating and there is no secure funding for conservation or staffing.

The collection is one of the best of its type in the country and its national importance has been recognised by experts from the National Museum of Photography, Film and Television. On a local level it offers an exciting insight into past life for children and newcomers to the area and is a wonderful source of nostalgia for older inhabitants. Despite its importance much of the collection will be lost without a large scale conservation programme and once lost these delicate images will be gone forever.

Lilian Ream in retirement, photographed by her grandson, Roger.